THE DARK SIDE OF AMERICA

THE AXIS OF EVIL IS NOT ONLY IN YOUR BACKYARD BUT IN YOUR FRONT YARD

By
Assefaw Habttie

Table of Contents

About the Author

Assefaw Habttie is a deeply reflective writer, cultural critic, and advocate for strong family values. Born and raised in Africa, Assefaw's journey has been one of resilience, transformation, and a relentless pursuit of understanding the complexities of human experiences across cultures. Having lived through the turmoil of displacement and the challenges of adapting to life in America, he brings a unique perspective that bridges worlds.

His lived experiences—from life in a refugee camp to working in diverse communities in the United States—inform his poignant and sometimes provocative commentary on societal structures, cultural conflicts, and systemic injustices. Assefaw writes with unflinching honesty, weaving personal anecdotes with sharp observations about the interplay of tradition, freedom, and accountability in modern society.

A strong advocate for preserving cultural heritage and family integrity, Assefaw uses his work to spark dialogue about the darker sides of undisciplined freedom, the flaws in legal and societal systems, and the erosion of respect in relationships. His thought-provoking narratives aim to shed light on issues often overlooked, particularly concerning immigrant experiences, racial inequities, and the universal desire for belonging and stability.

In "The Dark Side of Americans," Assefaw explores the contrasts between the opportunities and challenges of life in the United States, challenging readers to reflect on the cost of progress and the compromises made in the pursuit of individual freedoms. His voice resonates as a powerful testament to the courage it takes to confront uncomfortable truths and demand a better future for all.

Chapter One

Coming to America was good for only one reason: It brought safety from a bomb coming through your roof in the middle of the night. Of course, no one will deny that the United States is the place to be and the most powerful country in the world. You can be anything you want in the United States. Even if you were not born in the United States, you still can have the opportunity to work in high-ranking official government offices. In the United States, you have unlimited possibilities if you are willing to work hard and focus on it, but you must have a mindset rooted in belief.

If the mind can believe and conceive, the mind can achieve. Many smart and intelligent immigrants with this belief mindset have achieved and succeeded in living the American dream and holding higher positions of success. Many immigrants can come to the United States and be anything they want to become; they get the opportunity that they could never get in their own country.

The United States of America is the only country in the world that gives anyone the freedom to be what they want to be. No other country will provide you with the same opportunity as the United States. People from around the world, from different countries, want to come to the United States of America if they get the chance, and they all want the freedom that they can't get in their own country. Whether you are handsome, ugly, short, tall, or sick in the head, American will give you all the same opportunities you deserve. If you can make it, you get any position you earn and dreamed of.

Let me tell you something that no one knows and no one pays attention to, but I studied it so carefully, and not only that, but I have been collecting evidence and proof. Even though some, not all, but some white people are still black haters. They are not the only enemy of African American. Other immigrants look down on black people in America as well. But the ones most damaging the society and screwing up the American system are the immigrants.

White people are not that bad; most of the time, white people are humble, and their hearts are not that bad. Their mind or heart is not twisted, but most immigrants have bad and twisted hearts. These are the immigrants that have changed everything in America. When immigrants started playing games, taking advantage, manipulating the welfare, and committing fraud in the government benefits systems, then slowly, the white people started to get wiser to understand the twisted mind and recognized the fraud that most immigrants are playing games and making a living. It took many years for the white people to find out that the immigrants were playing a game with the system, and now the government makes it hard even to get approved for easy welfare. Also, the immigrants made the court system very hard. Many stupid wives, when they get to America, leave their husbands easily just because they want to express the freedom of America, so they drop their family just because the wife doesn't get things her way. The useless, materialistic, and dream-killer woman lies and manipulates the court system by lying to the judge. When the useless woman tells the judges a false story, she includes the culture of their hometown. To make the judge believe her, she tells lies, that men treat and see women less than men or they beat them and treated them badly back in their country, and the stupid judge easily and automatically believes the woman and makes the man and the kids' life very hard. Did you know that the immigrants are mean and rude to each other more than the white men are rude to us?

A selfish, useless woman doesn't allow the ex-husband to see the children, or she makes it incredibly difficult to get involved with the children and tries to take them far away. Sometimes, the mother does not allow the kids to go to their grandparents' house. She makes life difficult for that father who's trying to see his kids. Some of the single mothers are delusional. Then, the father doesn't want to dig deeper and deeper after so many times, and the father eventually gives up on the children. The stupid mother and selfish judge don't know or care about how the children and the father are going to suffer. A mother like this says she puts her ego above your emotional needs, knowing well.

Now that I have told you the true and good side of the United States, please allow me to tell you the dark side. Due to their high technology, sophistication, and too much freedom, this freedom leads them to be the most disrespectful, undisciplined country in the world. The United States of America. Not only that but the United States has contaminated and damaged many other countries with their undisciplined bad behavior. Many countries copycat the United States' bad behavior. I am not against women's rights, but hundreds of women escape from their country to the United States so that they can practice the freedom of the USA. I know many cases from the following countries: Dubai, Qatar, Somalia, Sudan, Saudi Arabia, Iraq, and many other countries. These women know that undisciplined American freedom can

protect them, and so they leave their own family and kids behind. And that's why they denied their own country and culture. Thousands of good married women with a strong cultural structure system come to the United States because of the undisciplined court system and the bad influence of American culture. Many marriages get divorced quickly due to the judgmental mindset of judges and selfish layers, like the woman's support organization.

Let me tell you something: just because some stupid American men abuse their wives, it doesn't mean all men are like that. So, when an immigrant, happily married couple comes to the USA and the wife makes a mistake in the marriage and asks for a divorce, the man is more likely to be blamed, and the access of the Evil court system always finds the husband is wrong. Most married immigrants find that the court is always on their side. They are not afraid to drop out and leave their marriage. I am not putting down all judges and lawyers. Let me explain and give an example of something about judges: Judges are in a closed position with limited information. They don't really have the time to try to solve and investigate the issues; they have thousands of cases to look at. So unconsciously and unknowingly, this makes them selfish and they don't really care and understand the real issue. At the same time, most of the judges don't understand how they affect society simply by not working hard on family cases. All they care is to go to the next case. Especially if they have not eaten lunch yet; studies show that if judges work on a case before their lunch, that case is in big trouble and more likely to be convicted wrongly. The judges don't really care; they just want to get it done.

Chapter Two

I wanted to tell you a story. I will not mention the place of the facility, but I worked in many retirement facilities, and I know thousands and thousands of stories but I will tell you only one. There was a man in his room, and he was in pain most of his days. I felt bad for him so I used to visit and check on him in his room. One day, he saw me coming in, but he didn't say anything. He was just staring through the window. I said Hello, how are you doing today? But he didn't respond. A few minutes later, he jumped and said Hi, Hoffa. I asked him what he was thinking about. He took a long pause and told me an amazing story. He said that a long time ago, about 39 years ago, he was working as a repo man, towing people's cars if they were behind on their car payments. He said that he regrets many cases but especially one case that he worked on haunted him even on his bed. He said that he had been looking for this woman's car for about a week, and finally, when he found the car he was looking for, he approached the woman and tricked and played a game on her by saying something was wrong in her car and having her open the trunk of her car. When she walked away from the driver's side to see the trunk of her car, he got into the car and let her know who he was, showed her the paperwork of repo and drove away with her car. Later that day, he found out that the woman was pregnant, and she had to go to the hospital and had a miscarriage due to the frightening situation that he caused by his action. He said that now it haunted him on his deathbed. I wondered how many nightmares some judges have on their deathbeds. Let me explain something: Just like doctors, they work and get paid by seeing patients. Don't forget they have bills to pay just like everyone else. Doctors don't have the time to do research for new diseases or study new medicine. On the other side, scientists discover new things. The same concept applies to judges. Most of the judges work behind closed doors. They are blind and don't investigate the truth. But some are Guardian Ad Litem, also known as a GAL. The GAL is sort of like a mediator between the two parties. The GAL digs out the right information and brings out the truth. However, not all GALs are as positive as I described; some GALs are haters and if they can get paid behind doors, they can manipulate the story. Since judge's work involves people's life, they should be really wise and careful when dealing with family matters. Their quick, judgmental work could damage innocent people's lives. It is destroying and separating families.

Also, did you know that many judges and lawyers who grew up in broken houses have been abused by their parents' fathers or, in some situations, by their mothers? They got out of it, and somehow, they made it to the school and became judges or layers. These people, instead of studying and investigating the situation carefully, quickly judge the situation by their awful memory and, in their small minds, put innocent people in jail or find them guilty just because they were treated badly by their parents. They think all men are the same. Those kinds of judges when they see a man in a courtroom, all they see and remember is their dad or the man who abused them as a kid, so they quickly find most men guilty.

Chapter Three

Where I come from, the court system doesn't work like this. The judges are not blind and don't get fooled. They never find someone guilty without investigating the issue. In Washington State, it is quite different. When a woman with no dream, a useless wife, accuses her husband of something, the judge automatically believes its' truth. Therefore, the father is perceived as violent, and he is ordered to take dozens of trainings on how to become a father/parenting class.

Many fathers quickly give up on life due to stress and frustration. In America, some state laws are selfishly designed to destroy low-income families and keep them in the lower-class life. The government has carefully designed an easy trap to keep the Black community in the lower class by providing easy access to food stamps and free housing. They make it difficult for the minority to get easy access to education and find a job. Many Black people are being deceived into this game and stay low class, ultimately affecting the next generations to come. Another issue is when a Black family faces a divorce, the court system is designed to discourage rather than reconnect the couple so that they won't be a successful family. What amazes me most is the selfish judges when they make their court judgments; they act as if they care about the kids and blindly side with ex-wife. When the selfish judge takes the wife's side, she really thinks the judge cares about her and the kids. With her total lack of foresight, she happily ditches her marriage and the father of her children.

Three years after the divorce, she learns how hard it is to be a single mother alone and raise kids. She really thought she could be both father and mother, handling and nurturing kids alone. She never thought what effect this would have on her kids with the father absent from their lives.

Soon, before she knows it, the kids are in bad shape. I am not saying all kids raised by single mothers will become bad. I realize that because Barack Obama was raised by a single mother. He became the first Black president of the United States of America. The majority of fatherless kids are missing a lot. Did you know that the most fatherless kids in the world are in the United States of America? Approximately about 19,395,00 children in the United States live without a biological father, and that is a very difficult life. Children who live in a fatherless home are about 85% more likely to deal with drugs and illegally carry a firearm. This is horrible, but the disturbing and hurtful part is what the kids are missing: not having the feeling of a father figure in their lives. The selfish mother doesn't care or can't figure out the kid's pain. The most painful thing is about 85% of youth in prison come from a fatherless home. Certainly, a woman cannot teach a boy how to become a man. It's not because she doesn't like her kids. She doesn't have the capability and the chemistry in her. A woman cannot teach her son how to swing a hammer or small things here and there. The most important part is the emotional absence is a silent killer that stays with the kids. As they grow up, they become a big man with weak "bones" and emotional distress. That is only in America; please don't take me wrong; there are many divorces in other countries, but they don't separate the kids from the father or mother, and they don't put strong restrictions on the father to see his kids just because the useless wife said so. Only the stupid judges in America set a restraining order for the father just because the women asked for it, especially in Washington.

Chapter Four

The most respected and the most disciplined marriage in the world is Muslim culture. But now, even Muslim wives have started to destroy and diminish their strongest cultural structure by divorcing their husbands when they come to the United States. That is all because of the undisciplined culture and too much stupidity of freedom in Americans. I don't want anyone to misunderstand me. We do have some divorce in other countries but not like the United States. I remember when I was a child, we used to say America was heaven. We only used to say this because some of the Muslim people used to take advantage of us and abuse us. When I say Muslim, I am only talking about the Bin Laden organization. Also, you must ask yourself what makes Bin Laden's organization hate American culture. Not all Muslim people are the same. This organization made us hate our lives, just like the White man makes Black people hate their lives here in the United States. I want to explain something about Muslim people. Not all Muslims hate Christianity. Actually, there are many Muslims who show sympathy and good feelings by helping and supporting Christians. I just ended up in a community of Muslims that was taken over by Bin Laden leaders. I remember there was a large refugee camp, and most of us were Christians and a little group of Muslims. Somehow, the Bin Laden group had lots of money, and they came and took over the community by helping the Christian people and converting them to a Muslim religion. Due to these conflicting and different beliefs, some Christians died, and some ran off. I remember in Sudan when I was living in the refugee camp, this group came into our town and burned our school to the ground. They killed many Christians. So, when the Bin Laden leaders used to tell us bad things about the United States, we believed what they were telling us was the truth. At the same time, we used to get confused when we saw the Red Cross come to our community and serve us food and milk. We all thought the United States was saving us.

We were very humble, and I only knew the good side of the United States. Now, I see and live things for myself and find out the truth. Yes, of course, America has a good side and an evil side.

Chapter Five

Many other countries in the world have amazing and strong cultural structures, but the US culture can be very brutal. In my African culture, as children, we never look straight into our parent's eyes when they are talking to us. We never looked straight into their face when they gave us any advice. We never reject any advice they give us. We never put or throw our clothes on the floor of our bedroom. We never let our elder sibling work or do something in the house while the younger is sitting around. We never respond to our parent's negative words or actions, but in the United States some kids not only don't listen to their parents, but they disrespect their own parents.

Where I came from, anyone in the community can discipline any kid even though they are not your parents. Anyone from the community can babysit your kids. Another example is standing up when we see anyone older than us. We jump to open the doors for older people. We give our seats and stand up for a person even if they are older than us by a month. We never eat without our parents at the table unless they are working and not home. We never bring our shoes inside of the house. We never allow our parents to do our work or pick up something while we are around them. We never reveal any story our parents have told us. We never let pets go on our beds or even inside our houses. Our pets have boundaries and have a special place made for them outside of our home and in the play yards. In most African countries, you can call your neighbor or someone from your community and ask them to do or to bring something for you.

An example is to bring you food or groceries or ask for simply milk or salt. Even if you don't know them that well, you might ask your neighbor to babysit your kids and they would be happy to help. That would be true in Asian countries as well.

In the United States, it is a completely different story. This kind of kindness in the United States sounds very strange and sometimes it's illegal even to ask. The scariest, shocking, weirdest, craziest, unbelievable, despicable, and disgusting thing that I will never understand and will never accept is the mental health system. If you are over eighteen years of age and have a mental illness, your family cannot tell you what to do. A family member may try to help them by keeping them in their house. If the child with a mental illness rejects your help, by law, you can't force them. If police become involved, you go to jail just for providing and trying to take care of your own child. Somehow, the smartest country in the world doesn't seem to understand this simple concept. The law can only act when a child with mental illness commits a crime. After it is too late, the government will want to do something. A long time ago, I heard this kind of sentence from Muslim leaders; I heard them say the United States will never take action to rescue a country from killing each other or civil war until it's too late. I didn't know they would play the same blind game to their own people. In my country, if someone has a mental illness, the entire community tries to help, and a family member will take care of the person. The government would never interfere unless you ask for help.

Chapter Six

I will give a very true story. At my work, I manage a group of about fifty-six staff. One of my employees had a child with mental illness. She used to come and tell me sad stories about her kid daily, and I used to send her home to care for the child. She said that the mental illness agency had released her child. The next day he ran out of the house, and she tried to get him from the street.

During this moment they both started to become loud and louder. She was begging her son to get into her car so that she could take him home. Someone was watching them from the parking lot and called the police on the mother. Of course, not all police are nice with warm hearts. In this incident, two heartless policemen arrived, and they told the Mother, she can't force her own son to come home. As the mother, she was screaming and crying for help. The useless, careless police officer let the eighteen-year-old kid walk away and told his mother not to chase her son. As the kid got farther and farther away, the mother kept arguing and begging the rude, heartless police officer to help her. When the police left, the mother tried to look for her son but couldn't find him. The Mother went home crying but never fell asleep all night. Somehow, the kid survived the night, but then, sometime around midday, she received a phone call from her neighbor who told her the bad news. Somehow, the child climbed on top of the roof and jumped. He broke his neck and died after being taken to emergency care. Until this day, I don't think the kid meant to kill himself; he was not suicidal. His mental illness was responsible for losing his life. The useless, mean police could have gotten out of their comfort zone and saved the kid's life. The police officer could have ignored some of the nonsense law structure and been nice to his community, but he didn't do that. In my strong opinion, the police were White, and the kid was Black. If the kid had been White, the police would have saved the kid's life. In my country, you can't find this kind of sad stories. If there is a situation like this, the police will not interfere unless asked to help. Our culture helps and supports each other. That Includes Muslim people who are great at helping each other in this kind of situation. Actually, Muslims have a strong cultural structure system and good discipline, except they are not nice to you if you are Black and Christian. Black people are pushed around. It doesn't matter where they live in this world. Did you know that Black Muslim people get treated badly by light-skinned people? That includes when people are in Mecca. Every year, over a million Muslims go to Mecca for Hajj just to touch the Black stone for less than five seconds, but Black Muslims have been pushed around until the rich Muslim people and light-skinned people have finished first.

Chapter Seven

In the United States, Black people live a worse life. This kind of situation happens daily due to the unspeakable racism that still exists and an undisciplined cultural structure. There is too much freedom. There are many differences in cultures. For example, in the United States, they don't handle death very well. If an American family loses a family member, they make a very short ceremony and are supposed to hide their grief. In our culture, it will take us weeks to bury the dead person. We have a large ceremony, and hundreds, even over a thousand people, come to visit the grieving family. To pay great respect, they all go to funerals. After the funeral they all gather again in a big hall and eat and pray together.

Did you also know in my culture, as well as in all African cultures, there is much concern about women's virginity? If a girl is getting married and the groom finds his bride, not a virgin, he will break the marriage immediately. The bride is taken back to her family. However, the groom must first do a big ceremony, spending thousands on the wedding while hoping the bride is a virgin girl. In the United States, they don't even care about whether the woman is a virgin or not. In some parts of Africa, marriage takes place without the bride and groom knowing each other. Their parents made a locked promise when their kids were as young as five years old, even two months old. In another part of Africa, the groom must kill a lion and bring the fresh, wet blood of the lion's skin and give it to the father of the bride. Then, the father gives his daughter to the man. So, when someone wants to get married, he has to go to a group of his friends and ask them to go with him to help kill the lion. It's so dangerous that six friends go out, and only three or four come back because they get killed by the lions or hyenas.

Another part of Africa has more than one wife. I used to live with Rashaida. Living with Rashaida is very relaxed with no stress at all.

They are very different from us. Men can marry up to three wives. If the man is rich and can afford the wives, all he must do is give money and two camels to the mother of the bride. If the man is poor and can't afford more wives, he must depend on his own daughters. He will hope and pray to have daughters so that he can exchange them for more wives. The sad part is that little girls must cover their mouths and face with niqab from the age of six to eight. The girls may then be married around twelve or fourteen.

I remember two of my Rashaida sisters got married while I was living with them. For the marriage, the family made a beautiful tent for the bride far away, around sixty feet, from her mom's house. When the moment comes, her mom and sister take her in the middle of the night, around 2 am, and leave her alone in the new tent. Then, around 3 am, the new husband comes and gets to meet her and have sex with her. She has never met the groom, but she knows his name. The next day, if the family is poor, they will kill one camel. If they are rich, they will kill two camels and enjoy the wedding and dancing.

Chapter Eight

I remember when we first came to the USA, I met a friend next door to where I used to live. This friend had been in the United States for a very long time, so he had taken on much of the American lifestyle. One day, when he came home, he brought me a game. We were playing the game in my bedroom. My mom kept coming to the bedroom door and asking me to get up and go to the store to get oil and milk. After she opened my bedroom more than three times and asked me to stop playing the game and go to the store, she was not happy. My friend with American style told me that it is your right and your personal space, and she can't do that. Tell her no and to wait until we finish the game. I looked into his eyes and told him I didn't want to get into trouble. I got up and went to my mom in the kitchen. I would never respond to my mom like that. The shocking thing is good culture comes to America and quickly goes bad. I can give you an example.

The American culture has an amazing, unspeakable issue with the age of 18 years. When kids reach 18 years of age, they are free to drink alcohol, and they can move out of the house. Due to this freedom, some kids can't wait to be 18 so that they have the dangerous fun and freedom of drinking. Some kids don't become alcoholics, but some of them never quit drinking. The law introduces drinking to the kids, and that is a bad idea!

I can give you another example. When I was in high school, in one of my classrooms, I had a teacher who had a cheetah picture on the wall. So, after class every day I used to stand and stare at the picture on the wall. After months, the teacher started to pay attention. She asked me why I stood and looked at the animal picture. I told her that this picture reminds me of where I came from. I asked her if I could have a copy. The teacher was so nice that she took the picture down and made a copy. She gave me the original, and she kept the copy for herself. The next day after class, I stayed in her class doing my homework since it was the last period. The teacher came to me and asked if I needed help. She helped me with my homework. From that day, every day I started to stay back in her class after school. I never knew that the teacher began to like me. One day, she took me to her house and had lunch, and then she dropped me off at my mom's house. Months went by, and she kept taking me to her house and feeding me. I used to tell her the story of my life in Africa. I started to help her around the house like washing her car and washing the dishes. Slowly, over time she started to touch me and give me a message. One day, out of nowhere, she took me to her bedroom, and I remember she called me "you little cute African tiger" and took off my clothes. It was my first sexual experience. I was so nervous, confused, and scared, but I managed. The next day, I was too scared to come to her class. Instead, I went to the library and sat there thinking about what happened. After class, many of my classmates told me that the teacher was looking for and asking about me. Somehow, she found out that I was at the school, so the teacher walked around and found me at the homework center. I remember she bent down and whispered in my ear. She said I know you are scared. I was so worried about you, and I am sorry I had to tell you something. Come to my class now. Slowly, I followed her to her class, and she grabbed me and kissed me. She said we must go home and she had something to show me. We went to her house. I was still nervous and broke down for some reason. I was feeling guilty or scared. We did it again. I can't say she raped me because I didn't run off from her, but she was doing all the sex and the action. I remember it was on Friday because the next two days I didn't see her at school. Then Monday came, and I went to the classroom but with my head down. I felt like everyone in the class knew something about what had happened. I couldn't even see anyone's face in the classroom. Many of the other students kept asking me if I had been in a fight or if I was sick. I kept answering them, no, I am fine. Then, after school my teacher told me she noticed everything that happened in the classroom. She told me not to act like this as it would get us into trouble. The students will think that you are too chicken or scary. After the end of the period, she took me home, and this time, I accepted the sex and started to go along with it. Seven to Eight months into the relationship, it was getting hard for me to meet her when she asked me to. I was so afraid that my family would find out. I never wanted to disappoint my mom, but I was even more scared of my older brother. He was in charge of the family at that time.

I remember she bought me a pager, and she said that when she wanted to see me, she would page me. Then I was to go outside my home to meet her. On top of me getting scared and being afraid my family would find out, it was also getting harder for me to maintain the relationship. When she paged me, I had to go to a payphone. Sometimes there was no good excuse to tell my family in order for me to go out of the house. I did this for over three months. It was so difficult to get out of the house and meet her. One day, I decided to end the secret pain and fear.

I threw away the pager and started to hide from her. One week after I disappeared, she started to come by my house and park in the hospital parking lot next to my house. She was watching me. One time, she convinced me to get into her car and go to her house. She asked me why I was not answering her page. I told her that my older brother knew and he wanted to talk to the church about you. She was surprised and shocked. The next day, I watched to see if she was around. I hid from her for another month, and finally, after two more months, she gave up, and I never saw her again.

Chapter Nine

I can give you another example. After I started to speak a little English and was in tenth grade, I had a Black American friend. He introduced me to another White kid. The White kid was very nice, and I was learning good English from him. Over time, we started to hang out together, and he started to like a Muslim girl from Afghanistan. Because I speak Arabic, I was telling him it would be hard to get her to date due to her religion. He would not give up, so I taught him a couple of Arabic words he could use to say hi to her. One morning, we met the girl in the hallway going to her classroom. He said hi in the Arabic language, and she was happy and responded with hello. From that moment, they started to talk and get to know each other. He explained to her that he liked her a lot. After four months, they were infatuated with each other. I remember she asked her family to work at McDonald's. At first, they said no, but then, somehow, she convinced them, and they gave her the ok. She used the MacDonald hours schedule to see her new boyfriend and she started to come home late. When I said late, I am not talking very late, as some American teenagers might do here in the United States. I am only talking about 45 minutes to an hour late from her normal hours. After three to four months, she completely started to ignore her family's rules. I grew up in the Muslim world; I knew something bad would happen soon. After she dated my friend for two months, he and I dropped her off late one night at her house. Her father saw us through the window. Right when she got in the house, I saw her being pulled by someone, who I thought was her father. I saw a second shadow come behind her, and then I saw her falling on the floor. I was not sure how hard she hit the ground. We drove away worrying about her. The next day she didn't come to school, and we never saw her again at the school. Students and teachers asked about her, but no one knew the answer. Even though I had a strong suspicion of what had happened to her, I was too afraid to speak up. Then, after four to five weeks, I started to really be worried about her, and I missed talking to her. I gathered up my courage and told one teacher the story. I am not sure if the teacher checked on her or not; I never heard back from the teacher.

After two years I was told somehow her parents took her back to their country. One day, she used her girlfriend's phone and sent me a picture of her. I asked and begged her friend if I could talk to her. The girlfriend said OK, but it took her about three weeks. It was hard because she got married back home, and she was afraid of getting in trouble again. After I talked to our old friend Zebiba, we both cried because it brought back all of the memories. Then she showed me bad bruises and old scars from what happened on that night. I remember my memory going back to that dark night. Zebiba, crying, told me the entire story. She said that her mom and father beat her. My first thought was I knew this was coming. I never knew that they would deport her back to her home country. The next word came out of her mouth I couldn't believe, and I couldn't believe what I saw. She said that her father used a knife, and her mother used a fork to cut all over her body as her father was saying (Yashakie, Fadahtini, Yashakie, Fadahtini) and kept stabbing her with fork and knife. She said she couldn't remember, but she thought she had fallen asleep. I don't think she was sleeping, just unconscious. As she finished telling me the story, I cried and felt very sad. I was sad about it for months.

I understood my good friend didn't know any better, but unintentionally, she was breaking and disrespecting her deep and strong culture structure.

Chapter Ten

Muslim culture has had a powerful hold on its followers for thousands of years. When Muslim people come to the United States, some of them let go of the strong culture that they have been practicing for thousands of years. Another example is most Muslim women must cover their hair, and some of them even cover part of their faces so you can only see their eyes. Now, many Muslim people are getting divorced due to some women not following their original culture. Some women are breaking their original culture that has been respected for thousands of years. Many families come to the United States with a strong, respected culture, but then when they get to the United States, their wives say this is America and give attitude. They change their behavior and end up getting divorced, and this is because of the undisciplined cultural structure of America. I know many true stories that many families with strong and respectful cultures come to the United States. The wives changed their minds and asked for a divorce. They know there is this sad opportunity for single mothers. The undisciplined and careless court system will help single mothers to raise their kids without a father. If this undisciplined, careless court system were not in place, women coming from other countries would not act or destroy their families' values. When a Black family comes to the court for divorce issues, 95 % of judges will not put the family back. As a matter of fact, some judges pray for Black families' cases. Some think in their mind, "Here is another Black family to destroy," because they know if Black kids grow up fatherless, they will end up in drugs and crime, and the broken family will keep going for generations. Before it gets fixed or cleaned up, the Black families are way behind. This is how 90% of judges in the United States structure the court system to put down, push, and delay Black people's society in low-life living.

I know seven to eight real stories. Many newcomer wives from other countries know America has freedom of speech. They understand most of the time the law is on their side. Not all women, but some useless wives know if they cause an issue with their husbands, the court system will support them. Therefore, it's easy for the wives to disrespect their husbands and destroy their marriages. I know a couple who got married after they brought their new fiancé to the United States. The wives changed their attitudes and behavior and changed their minds about being with their husbands. These wives got the information from families and friends, and finally, they asked their husbands for divorce. When the husband was against the divorce, the wife talked to family and friends for their advice. I can give a true example of a useless wife that I know.

She didn't want to be with her husband seven months after she got to the United States. She changed her mind about her husband so she started trouble with him. The wife began to talk negatively to friends, and they advised her to take the kids and go to a shelter. Then, the shelter will immediately get her the help that she wants. Knowing this information, many useless wives went to the shelter, taking the kids with them. They used the children as a tool to escape the marriage and ask for help. The useless newcomer wife does not know how hard it is to be a single mother in the United States. She missed the big picture, destroyed the families' values, and raised the poor kids without a father. This is a very true story and growing behavior in the United States. The United States doesn't have strong family and marriage values. They should not make it easy for a useless wife to take advantage of the system. Many women know this system exists in the United States, so they get married to a hard-working man just to get to the United States. Many women from other countries know the United States court system is too easy for women. Therefore, they are desperate to get married to anyone who is a US citizen so that they can use them to get to the United States.

Chapter Eleven

We used to hear all this bad and dark side of the United States in the refugee camp from the Bin Laden organization.

The Bin Laden organization Muslim people used to teach us the United States is very nasty and has dangerous people. The people in the United States will compare us to dogs, and they might even have more respect and care for dogs than the immigrant people from Africa. Don't hope to go to the United States. As kids, we really wondered about what to believe when they said this. The Bin Laden organization used to teach us everything was the opposite about the USA. We never believed their story. We thought they said this because the Bin Laden group hated the United States so much.

The Bin Laden organization used to tell us how women in the United States didn't cover their hair and dressed inappropriately to look sexy. They told us American women are very cheap and dirty. The Bin Laden group taught us that American men put their women in Playboy videos. We never believed them. As a child, we were so confused because we saw the White people from the Red Cross helping us with food and other good things. At the same time, the Bin Laden organization was teaching us the opposite side, so we were completely confused and lost.

When I came to the United States, I got to see things myself. I found out most of the things that I used to hear were absolutely true.

American infidelity is almost normal. Many marriages or other relationships are broken due to disrespect for each other by cheating. Due to this kind of behavior, many families live separately, and about forty-one percent of all first marriages end in divorce. Many single mothers depend on the government support. Kids grow up fatherless and, in their teens, fall into problems. Many fatherless kids get into issues like alcohol or drugs and end up in jail and charged as criminals. The broken family pattern continues through time and will take many generations to fix.

I know for a fact many judges like to keep the Black families destroyed. When a Black family comes to the court for divorce, some racist and hater judges are very excited to see them for one reason. They want to destroy the Black families and take every opportunity to do so. All they think is 'Here goes another back family to destroy. Instead of trying to get counseling, no one works to get them back together with their kids. These kinds of judges design their court system to damage and destroy the Black family by making it hard for the husband and easy for the wife. The woman really thinks the system cares about her but has not seen the deep root of the destroyed family. Many respected, disciplined, and well-organized cultures come to the United States, but then, after a few years the family gets destroyed and broken. Take a divorce case, for example. The new, well-organized family lives happily until the wife learns the many deceiving ways, and it looks like an opportunity. Many fake rules are designed to destroy the family, and the foolish woman falls on it. When the selfish judge takes her side and rules in her favor, she really thinks the judge cares about the family or the kids. When foolish women see this fake deal, they believe there is help for them. Many of the women quickly decide to get a divorce. The undisciplined American freedom gives the newcomer a new attitude very quickly. Unfortunately, this is only designed to destroy her family. She thinks she is getting help from the court system.

I don't mean to disrespect the Christian religion, but because of the marriage system, over 55% of Christian religious believers are living divorced. Nowadays, even in the most powerful and respectful culture, Muslim wives are leaving their husbands because they know the stupid, selfish gene court system will just take their side no matter what.

Chapter Twelve

Many women see and acknowledge this with no big reason. If they are not happy or things do not go their way, they just start disrespecting their husbands and file for divorce. Many happy wives end up breaking their families by believing the court system will give them freedom.

A few years after the divorce, half of the women regret to start living empty with no real value in life. Also, many of them live in hardship and end up single rest of their life. Men, on the other side, never want to get married again.

Women really think the Judge cares about them, but I am going to tell you the real truth: 90% of all judges don't care about you or the kids. Think about it: what does the Judge know about their work? As much as I hated the bad cops, but still, they were still better than the stupid, selfish gene judge who sat at his little dark desk. What do they really know or see for them to make the right judgment? They only go by what others have told them, make their stupid, quick judgment, and go on to the next case. Real judges will take time and effort to study and investigate the case before they put people's lives in jeopardy. I am speaking from seven real experiences. One example, I had my best friend go through a divorce, and the stupid wife accused him of hitting her. I know for a fact he did not hit her, but the selfish gene judge believed her story and punished the man for no reason. The wife had a change of mind to leave her husband after she used him to get to the United States.

So, I have some advice for you all. If you want a real life with a wife, don't ever bring your wife to America. I don't care how she talks to you to get her to the United States or try to convince you that she will never change or be disrespectful to you or her marriage; don't believe that. No matter what, when they get to the US, they will change. Sometimes, it's not their own fault. It's the stupid, selfish gene court system that makes their minds change to have a happy family. The United States is only good for two reasons: No bomb will come above your roof, and the second one is you can become what you want to be, going to school or business.

Otherwise, if you want to be married and have family in America, literally your life is like a Gorilla's life. Let me explain: Gorilla lives happily with his large, happy family. Then, another larger Gorilla comes and attacks the father. The father will not only lose his wives but also the entire family, including his kids, become the new Gorilla kids. So, anytime when the useless wife asks for a divorce, the husband loses.

In many cases, the useless, trashy wife accuses the husband, and the selfish gene Judge takes her side and makes it hard to see his own kids, and many kids grow fatherless. Unless the trash wife is on drugs and is dragging the children, and that is with strong evidence.

Chapter Thirteen

The most people I respect in this world, besides my mother and my kids, are the Black people of the United States. There is no price high enough to pay for what Black people have done for us to have life in America. If it weren't for Black people who went through slavery in the United States, no one in America would have what they have right now. The Black people in America cleaned up for all the immigrants to have a life in the United States. I truly believe in my heart if it weren't for Black people, we would not have this life in America. They paid the price for us to have this life. Actually, I could have died a long time ago if it weren't for Black people. I can't even express or explain what Black people paid for us to have what we have right now. That includes some White people, too. The reason I say this is because if Black people didn't pay the price, the United States system would still be corrupt and would be the dumbest country still practicing slavery.

Being Black in America is very hard. Black people pay a heavy price for little crime. Many Black kids get punished around, but for the same crime, White kids get no criminal charge or even taken to jail. Although America is the greatest country in the world, the darkness and shamelessness will never be forgotten or erased.

Let me tell you the dark side of America. Many people in the world think America is free, but America is a jail. America is the meanest and cruelest evil doing of history in the world.

Black Americans have historically faced discrimination and even abuse by medical professionals, issues that have again come to the forefront during the pandemic. I hear from Americans who have directly experienced discrimination. For many years, I have worked in retirement living assistance, where I love talking to the elderly and asking them historical questions. White Americans used to practice medicine and experiment on Black people. White people used to force Black people to sleep and have sex with their own parents so that they could multiply for slavery values, which allowed them to sell more slaves. Sometimes, I ask myself where was God when this happened. The White enslavers who did medical experiments on Black people will go straight to real hell. White people make some Black people hate themselves and change their identity. Many Black people in the United States became Muslim only because White men made them hate themselves. Black people found out the biggest enemy of White people in this world was the Muslims, so Black people started to join and convert to Islam. What do Black people in the United States know about the religion of Islam? The only way to isolate and find a group is with the Islam religion. Some of the Black people might not admit this but that is the real truth.

Chapter Fourteen

Not all, but some American people have an insecure and selfish gene. People in the United States are so insecure and don't trust each other. As my mom used to say, "Too much of anything is not good for you and or will kill you." The United States has so much freedom and undisciplined culture in its court system, even though every day, they kill each other with their own guns. For many years, the United States government could not fix its gun law problem. Gun issues have been a very long battle for their culture. In the United States, gun violence is so bad that little innocent kids die in their schools every day, and the problem still not be solved, even now. My heart grieves for the innocent kids who have to die. They believed the safest place that they thought was the learning building. The United States stands out for its high levels of gun violence in the entire world. In the United States, every day, about 322 people are shot, and among those, 111 are shot and killed.

Each year, more than 39,000 people in the United States die as a result of gun violence, and tens of thousands more suffer non-fatal gun injuries. Gun violence in the United States has affected people of all ages and races in the U.S. but has a disproportionate impact on young adult males and racial/ethnic groups. The United States spends $280 billion on gun violence annually. The United States fights its battle due to costs of firearm assault injury, including work loss, medical, mental health care, emergency transportation, police, criminal justice activities, insurance claims processing, employer costs, and decreased quality of life. Gun violence is preventable, but the big guys don't really care to fix it, and it's unfixable. Gun violence is not inevitable.

Also, some American parents are not careful about gun safety. They give easy access to youth and children; I have known about ten cases in the state where I lived.

In 2020, Congress provided $23.5 million to the National Violent Death Reporting System to fund all 50 states, even if that will never fix the gun violence in the United States.

On top of their gun control issue, the United States can't even solve their own nightmares as they try to police the world.

The United States goes around the world and tells other countries what to do or tries to control the war between different countries. For example, if the United States wanted to stop the Ukraine war, they could, but they didn't want it to stop, and that's why it is still going on now.

I can only wish for 4 things to change in the United States:

Gun control Laws: Many innocent kids take their potential and dreams to the grave because some stupid adults can't fix the gun issues.

Selfish Gene Judge: Educate the stupid, selfish gene judges to do their job right and do it based on hard evidence, not their childhood memories. Just because they had bad experiences with their own fathers, they don't have to destroy other families.

Racism: Hard punishment for racist people so that no one will repeat it. Watch the song (This is America). It will explain the past, present, and future of America.

Marriage laws: Change the dirty marriage law! When a useless, trashy wife with no dreams wants a divorce, just let her go empty; don't give her half of the man's belongings that she didn't earn. Some women destroy their families just to get half of their husbands' money and benefits. If the stupid court system practices this, the divorce rate will drop, and kids will not be fatherless and stay out of trouble. The funny and hilarious thing is American court system doesn't have any respect for family values when it comes to divorce, but then they give more respect to animals. How are you going to have respect for animals when you don't respect a human being like you? That is fake.

By Assefaw Habttie